Walks from your car

CW00802015

Grange, Cartmel and the Lyth Valley

by
Ian Brodie

Dalesman Books
1989

Introduction

THIS BOOK encompasses walks in the south east corner of the Lake District National Park as well as in the attractive Cartmel peninsula outside the park boundaries.

These are footpath rather than fell walks although one or two minor summits are included. They are walks through relative quiet areas where the masses that believe the Lakes begin at Windermere stream past in their cars – the people who are ignorant of the microcosm of the national park and Cumbrian countryside held within these intimate but parochial dales. They are walks for the family and for the discerning rambler.

The book is unique in another respect. All the routes have, prior to publication, been the subject of consultation with the two relevant public authorities who have responsibilities for public rights of way, Hopefully this will result in the removal of any possible footpath obstructions before you venture forth. Many thanks thus to George Flynn of South Lakeland District Council and John Capstick and David Thomas of the Lake District Special Planning Board. If you do encounter any problems en route please let these authorities know.

The book has been written with the co-operation of my wife, Krysia, who has walked these routes with me and Joan and Paul Tolcher who have acted as guinea pigs in pre-testing the routes.

Ian O. Brodie

The Dalesman Publishing Company Ltd.,
Clapham, Lancaster, LA2 8EB

First published 1989

© Ian Brodie, 1989

ISBN: 0 85206 966 9

Printed by Swannack Brown & Co., Ltd., Hull, England.

Contents

Cover map by Barbara Yates

Ayside – Bigland Hall – Seatle – Ayside

THIS walk takes us into some delightful countryside that has some superb views but uses a very quiet part of the National Park. The walk is some 7-8 miles and footwear will be determined by some wet patches underfoot.

We start on the A590 just above the village of Ayside at the road junction opposite Whitestones Caravan Site (between Newby Bridge and Newton).

There is room to park by the junction at grid reference 391841 on O.S. map SD28/38 Broughton & Newby Bridge, which you should carry.

A stile and footpath sign by the west side of the road junction leads you into a field which you should cross below the steeper, bouldery section, then cross a stile in the fence and then down a stile in a wall and then over a stile by a gate.

Go down the next field by the right-hand wall to a stile and footbridge on the bottom left-hand corner of the field. Over this follow the left-hand boundary up the field, cross the road and, using stiles, the next field to enter a wood.

The path goes up through bracken in the wood (bluebells earlier in the year), then go left when you meet a wider track to meet a stile where the fences join. Leave the wood by the gap facing you and cross the field by the old hedge line to a stile by a holly and to a stile, across the next field, in the hedge.

Go right along the road, with the views of the Coniston fells and Windermere, to re-enter the field on your left through the second gate.

Cross to a gate and then to the left of a barn to find a gate by the overhead wires. Cross and follow the right-hand wall to the corner of the field where, if a stile has been erected, you can cross the wall facing you, (otherwise use a gate further along but come back to your right).

Over go left on the track but after a few yards strike right up the field

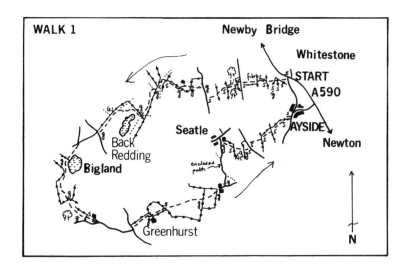

WALK 1

Newby Bridge

Whitestone

START

A590

Seatle

AYSIDE

Newton

Back
Redding

Bigland

enclosed
path

Greenhurst

N

with a beck over to your right to reach a gate. Through this go left using a rough track that keeps near the left-hand wall and eventually reaches a small gate and footpath sign at the far end of this large enclosure.

Through go right and follow the track near the right-hand wall and above Back Reddings/Black Beck Tarn-part of Bigland Hall sporting estate. The path cuts the right-hand corner of the enclosure and again follows near the right-hand wall to a further footpath sign.

Keep along the right-hand wall and go down to the road by a gas pumping station. Along this section are good views into Lakeland. Cross the road to the right and go through the gate posts and down the track towards Bigland Hall and Tarn, keep left at the junction to go by the tarnside path.

From the gate at the far side go to the marked track climbing the short hillside towards Grassgarth with super views of the Leven estury. Follow this waymarked route over the col and by a gate down through a wood, largely oak coppice, to re-emerge by a gate. Through here go near the left-hand wall and then through the garden of Grassgarth to follow their access track to the road. Go left on the road to the junction.

Facing you is the entrance to Greenhurst, go through and down the drive to the gate just above the farm. Do not go through this but instead use the gate to the left. Go by the right-hand wall eventually down to a gate in the bottom corner. Through go down the next, large enclosure keeping right but very gradually leaving the right-hand wall to find a gate in a fence.

A track continues down and at the junction go left to reach High Cark Hall farmyard. Pass through the yard, go along the road and left, through a gate, at the first junction. This leads down an enclosed track which bends and eventually goes narrower to emerge on the road just below the delightful hamlet of Seatle.

Just before your enclosed track ends is a small barn. Leave your track here to the right, go down the field near the left-hand boundary, through the gap (a stile should be erected a little further on) and then down the thin woodland with the clearing on your left.

Leave to woodland at a gate where the wall gives way to a hedge, Cross the field directly to a stile and go left along the road. A footpath sign and stile some 50 metres upon your right re-admits you to the field. Go down to a stile in the wall between the fence and hedge and then follow the right-hand wall over a stile in a fence, over the rise and down to a stile.

Over continue in the same direction with the wall on your left until a marked stile crosses you over this boundary.

From here go right to a stile by a gate and then left through Ayside, left at the junction to regain your starting point.

Walk 2   **6 miles**

Grange-over-Sands – Hampsfell – Cartmel – Grange

THIS walk begins at Grange-over-Sands railway station (grid ref. 412782 on OS Sheet SD 37/47 Grange-over-Sands, which should be carried) and visits Hampsfell and Cartmel before returning to the start in its 6 mile saunter.

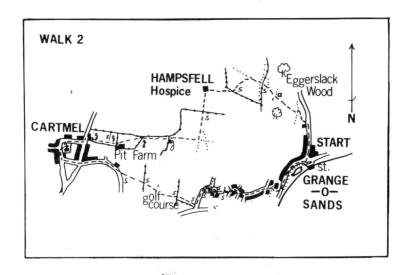

WALK 2

HAMPSFELL Hospice

Eggerslack Wood

N

CARTMEL

Pit Farm

golf course

START

St. GRANGE —O— SANDS

Grange was chosen as the start because it serves rail, bus and car travellers. Cars can be parked near the station in Windermere Road.

From the station go forward, passing the ornanmental gardens and famous duck pond, to the garage and right into Windermere Road. Follow the pavement until it ends at a footpath sign (Hampsfield – being the correct name of Hamspell) on your left.

The path climbs gradually through Eggerslack Wood and is well signed until it emerges on the open fell through a stile in the wall. A short Nature Trail Guide can be purchased in Grange to accompany you on this first part of the walk. The way crosses a track and at the second such crossing go slightly left. Ignore all side tracks but make sure you keep to the left branch just before the stile in the wall.

With your back to the stile follow the track onto open land and after a few strides, go climb to the right hand side of an overhead wire pole and then continue up the fell towards the left-hand wall which you will meet at a stile some 30m before it bends sharp right.

Follow the wall when over the stile and when it bends away climb the fell ahead and the famous shelter, the Hampsfell Hospice, soon comes into view. The extensive views of the Lakes, Yorkshire Dales and seaward Lancashire can be enjoyed as well as more local views of the Kent Estuary and Morecambe Bay with the viewfinder on top, or the riddle inside can be solved.

The views indeed are magnificent and a clear day adds much to the character of the walk and to the effort of the short climb.

From the shelter, continue your walk in the direction of Morecambe Bay, more particularly to the right aiming for Heysham Nuclear Power Station and the penisula that holds Humphrey Head. Go down to the wall to find a track and stile.

Over the stile follow the distinct track ahead and, when it comes towards the dip, bear right and then in the dip go right to descend on a narrower path that leads in the direction of Cartmel with its priory and backdrop of Mount Barnard with the Leven Estuary and Chapel Island beyond.

Go down, with the overhead wire pole on your right to meet a kissing gate in the wall across your way. Through follow the right-hand wall to a signed gate and, in the following field, go to pass the right-hand side of the farm buildings.

Behind the buildings is a gate and stile. In the field follow the left hand boundary over to meet a gate and short enclosed path between the houses.

On the road go left but then turn right to reach the churchyard by an outlying part of Cartmel village. Go through the yard to the front gate.

You have time to explore the Priory and the village.

To continue turn left along the road outside the front gate of the Priory and left at the first junction with its old signpost from the days when the stage coaches crossed the esturaries.

Cross the next junction (still signed Grange) and climb past the houses and, after the final dwellings where the road bends right, to a stile and signpost on your left.

Enter the field and follow to the right of the overhead wires as you climb steeply. Cross under the wires at right angles to you and continue to the field boundary across the top of the field to a stile which admits you to the golf course.

Go to the right of the tee and follow the thin path up to a track to pass a "ladder" and then along a line of fir trees to pass between a tee and a green to reach a stile that enables you to leave the golf course.

In the field, follow the right-hand fence along and down to a stile in the far right-hand corner. Through go left up the lane and to a stile in the wall on your right by a footpath sign (opposite the first gate on the left after the covered reservoir). Go down the small field to the left of the house and then right on a track that descends to a farm. When the track bends right into the yard a stile near the building on your left re-admits you to a field.

Follow the right-hand wall over the field and after the next stile follow the right-hand tall wall of a garden as the path goes down to a road.

Go first left but keep right where the next two tracks go off left to reach a further meatalled road. Go left and continue straight on when the wider road goes right (by a seat on the left). At the bottom of the hill go left and then right at the footpath sign. Follow the path left and down in the woods to pass through the gardens of the former Yewbarrow Lodge and down to the ornamental gardens in Grange near the start.

Walk 3   **6 miles**

Cartmel – Holker – Leven Estuary – Cark – Cartmel

A WALK of 4 to 6 miles – depending on your inclinations – that offers a gentle stroll coupled with some fine estuary scenery. Boots are only needed after vey wet weather. Holker Hall and Park can be visited.

Starting at the entrance to the car park at Cartmel Race Course (grid ref. 377797 on OS 37/47 Grange-over-Sands, which you should carry), having paid your conscience car park fee, there is a footpath sign from the gateway to Well Knowe. Follow the path over the course, past the left-hand side of the cricket square and to a stile in the rails on the far side of the course to enter a wood. Note the Silurian rocks underfoot that contrast to limestone in Cartmel village buildings.

Climb up the most obvious path through the trees and, bearing left at the fork after the steep climb, leave the wood by a gap stile. Follow the right-hand wall to emerge on a road by a further gap stile.

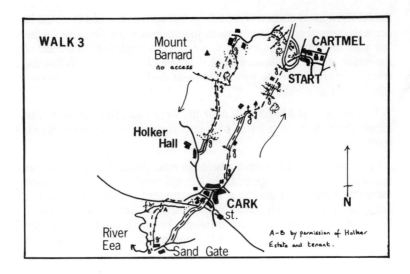

WALK 3

Mount Barnard ▲
no access

CARTMEL

START

Holker Hall

CARK
st.

N

A—B by permission of Holker Estate and tenant.

River Eea

Sand Gate

Turn left on the road, pass Walton Hall Farm and come to a sign for High Mill House and a footpath sign to Mount Barnard. This latter is somewhat misleading as the top third of this 'Mount' is out of bounds. This distinctive knoll is where it is said the monks who established themselves at Cartmel were intending to build their monastery.

The track bends left to a pass a bungalow and house before a gate, with its typical Holker cautionary sign, admits you to the wood. Take the obvious track that climbs across the hillside and eventually levels before descending slightly to a further gate which you use to leave the wood.

In the field follow the track by the right hand wall all the way down to a gate and cattle-grid with views of Morecambe Bay ahead. Go over the cattle-grid, ignoring the plethora of tracks and paths, to go down to the B5278 road outside Holker Hall.

Go left, using the pavement to pass the entrance to Holker Hall and Park. If you intend to use this visit to see the hall and park, please note they are closed on Saturday.

Continue along the road and, just after Cark Manor, turn right down the road. At the junction at the bottom go right but cross the footbridge with its footpath sign. The bridge crosses Mill Race which is really the

River Eea from Cartmel.

Over the bridge go right to follow the river under the railway, through the right-hand of two gates and emerge on the estuary saltings. The best time is a t high tide on a clear day if views to the far Furness shore are to be fully appreciated.

Go left along the edge of the saltings to reach Sand Gate where the shrimpers take to the sands. (This is not a public right-of-way, but the landowner and tenant have given permission for its use – as has permission to use part of the saltings). Go along the road until a footpath sign on your left (to Cark-in-Cartmel) allows you to follow an enclosed lane that eventually leads to Cark (ignore footpath signed to Cark Manor on left) and gives extensive views.

On your way into the village, the path crosses the railway on a very impressive bridge. Go right at the junction and then left over the bridge by the Engine Inn.

Go along the road but take the Cartmel branch at the junction and continue along this road until you leave the last house of the village – the impressive old Cark Hall with stupendous chimneys, an attractive front and mullioned windows.

Just after the house, a gated track goes off to the left. Follow this, pass above Low Bank Side Farm and, with attractive views of Hampsfell in front, continue to a gate at a junction.

Go right down a gated track that leads through a wood, down an enclosed lane and across a large field to reach the race course at Cartmel. For those who do not know the area, refreshments are available in Cark and in Cartmel and the latter village and Priory are well worth visiting.

The walk could of course have been cut shorter by keeping on the B5268 and missing out the estuary section – but your walk will be poorer for so doing.

Flookburgh – Leven Estuary – Flookburgh

FLOOKBURGH, our starting point, is named either from a fish (Flock, Floe) or from the common Norse personal name Flok – dating from the tenth or eleventh centuries.

During the plague the local population was devastated to such an extent that there was not enough inhabitants remaining to carry the dead to Cartmel. Instead they used two large, local excavations.

Start from the square in Flookburgh (only a short walk from Cark-in-Cartmel railway station). (Grid ref. 367758 on OS SD37/47 Grange-over-sands, which should be carried). Cars can be parked in the square around the signpost which is mounted on a memorial base stone of Flookburgh church and reads "St John the Baptist built 1777 taken down when the new church was built."

The signpost sits incongruous on the site of the original church that was too small to serve the local population. The site became derelict before becoming part of the local highway in 1925.

Flookburgh is noted for its fishing industry and two sections of the walk are on ways the fisherman take their tractors onto the estuary sands. King Edward I stayed locally on his way to hammer the Scots. Whether he gained vigour from the cockles is unknown but the taste impressed him enough to give Flookburgh a market charter.

Leave the square by Main Street and follow the metalled lane as it leaves the village to climb and then descend to the aptly named Sand Gate.

Passing through the village, you will notice the many seventeenth century cottages. These are fortunate to remain for it is recorded that in 1686 "a careless housewife" caused a fire that devasted 22 properties.

From the rise before Sand Gate there are extensive views of the Leven estuary, Chapel Island, Ulverston, Harter Fell and the Coniston fells. Chapel Island can be reached from Sand Gate but it is essential that tide tables and the local guide (tel Ulverston 54156) are consulted. Add a good 4 miles onto the total for the walk.

Go to the shore and turn left. Here the River Eea joins the sea – a river that 3 miles earlier passed through Cartmel as a placid backwater.

Keep along the shoreline by the edge of the field boundaries, over a bridge and reach a stile beneath the eroded red clay cliffs of Lenibrick Point.

Continue along the shore to reach the side of Canon Winder Farm with its mixture of square and round chimney pots and mullioned

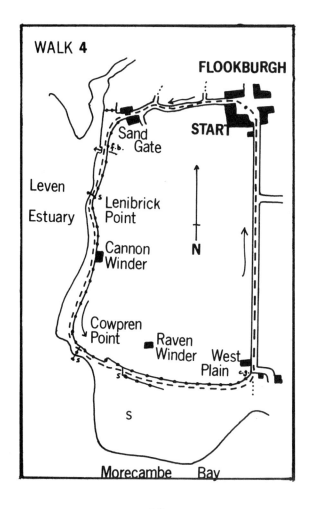

windows. Flowers along the shore include yellow horned poppies, feverfew, silverweed and pineapple mayweed (crush and smell).

Continue along the shore until Cowpren Point is reached and where the left-hand boundary swings east. Go over the stile and continue to follow the left-hand boundary.

At Cowpren Point the local fishermen can be watched at low tide, or the racing tide and sea at flood. Here, where the ebb was once chased with horse and cart to the cockle beds, now the tractor-seated fisherman goes for shrimps and flukes. Birds of many varieties can be seen as can Piel Castle. As we turn we begin to view the extent of Morecambe Bay.

A wire fence crosses the path but a stile allows access to the embankment which is followed to the metalled road and cattle grid at West Plains Farm.

The salt marsh to the right was once considered as the site of a reservoir for people of North West England. Ahead lies the whale back of Humphrey Head, to its left and more distant, lies Arnside Knott and, across the bay, the heights of Ward's Stone and the Forest of Bowland moorland.

The shapes of Heysham Nuclear Power stations lie across the sands which described as "the majestic plain where the sea has retired".

By turning left along the road you can follow its straight mile to Flookburgh and where its grass verge will relieve the footslog. The shop of the local fishermen is also passed as is the remains of Cark airfield where parachustists return quietly to earth in contrast to the nagging drone of the plane that takes them skyward.

Lindale – Hampsfell – Lindale

HAMPSFELL is a lump of Carboniferous limestone that runs down to the shore of Morecambe Bay at Humphrey Head. As in an earlier walk, the hill is often seen as synonymous with Grange. The fell does shelter the inhabitants of Grange from the worst of the north and westerly winds but to simply regard it as Grange's fell ignores the claims of Cartmel and of Lindale.

Northwards, the ridge continues into Lakeland by way of the Silurian rocks of Newton Fell and Hampsfell itself is part of the outer rim of Lakeland limestone – indeed the National Park boundary crosses the fell without any respect for landscape quality. As Hampsfell is thus integral to Lakeland it should be climbed from a Lakeland village, Lindale.

Start from Lindale Church (grid ref. 414803 on OS SD48/58 Milnthoepe – the walk also needs SD28/38 and SD37/47 of the OS Pathfinder series) but please don't park there if a service is to take place. The church is reminiscent in style of Lakeland dale churches but its size and steep hillside site add to its nature.

From the road above the church turn left and then right into Lingarth Estate. The newer houses to the left show how a sensitive approach from the local authority can help the character of a Lakeland village.

The road goes up through the estate and then becomes a path. Cross over the lane that comes next to some stone steps and then enter the field to climb up by the left-hand wall to some further steps.

From this field, extensive views of Morecambe Bay, the Forest of Bowland, Arnside Knott, Ingleborough and the Howgills are already opening.

From the steps cross the private drive to an old gate post and descend through the trees to a kissing gate and field. Go to the far right-hand corner of the field to a small gate and gap stile. In the next field, go across to a gate that leads to the gap between the house and former farm buildings seen ahead.

Please note at this stage the way you have come as this will also

15

form the final section of your return to Lindale.

Through the buildings follow the metalled road until it bends right below Redriggs with the post box by the barn. Go left by the gated track and down a short lane to a farm. Immediately after the first building on your right turn right and go through the gated yard that becomes an enclosed lane.

One visit here showed that bracken was being cut for use an animal bedding. The lane gives good views ahead towards Caw, the Coniston fells and Langdale Pikes.

Through the gate at the end of the lane follow the tracks across the

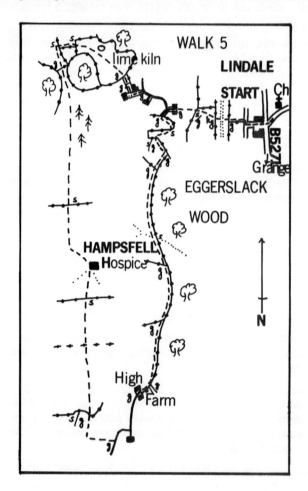

field to pass through a narrowing of the field where, on your right, a walled enclosure holds a large lime kiln.

From here follow the left-hand hedge and wall until it bends away to the left. Now aim for the middle of the wall ahead to find a stile some 10m from the right-hand of two gates.

In the next field follow the left-hand hedge and wall to a gated gap stile just away from the field corner. Descend from the stile, turn left, and follow the left-hand wall to a gate in the corner of the field.

Through, follow the gently rising path that follows the right-hand wall for about 100m before gently climbing with the dark green conifers to your left.

As you proceed along the open fellside the view of Cartmel and its Priory and vale open up to a wider view of the Leven estuary. The path is distinct on the ground and in early summer many flowers can be seen, it leads to a gate and stile over which you continue with the higher limestone escarpment to the left and, looking back, a whole vista of Lakeland fells from Black Combe to High Street can be seen.

When the next wall that crosses your way comes into view, strike left up the limestone to reach the building, Hampsfell Hospice. The limestone pavement on the left is probably the highest point of the 240m (727') high Hampsfield Fell. The shelter, with its top mounted viewpoint indicatior, was provided by a Cartmel clergyman for "the shelter and entertainment of travellers over the fell".

Inside the drafty limestone building are boards of verse dated 1846 which tell you how to behave, set you a riddle and provides an answer.

From the hospice walk towards the point of land, Humphrey Head, that juts into Morecambe Bay, to pick up a path that passes a large cairn to reach a stile in the wall. Setting the indicator at 200° tells you the correct direction.

The view in front is superb but don't miss the odd, darker rocks. These glacial erratics came from further north in Lakeland. Pass through a gap in a ruined, darker stone wall that marks the National Park boundary, and go down to a path junction in a gap on teh fell. Go left and contour around the hillock facing you and then descend to a gate and stile in the wall facing you. For the first time the skyline of Grange is visible.

Through the gate continue in the same direction to reach a depression with a large pile of stones at its top. Turn left here and, with the hollow on your right, go down to a gate, through which lies a track.

Go left along the track, keep left at Spring Bank and eventually pass through the gated yard of High Farm. Through, under the overhead wires, is a gate and footpath sign to your right – your way lies on the track and right-hand wall on this side of the gate.

Follow this wall for over a mile, passing through three gates and with Eggerslack Wood also to the right.

After the third gate the track bends left – continue to follow the wall until a further gate gives access to a wood. The wall is now on your left as you climb slightly right into a wood (this is signed). A wall meets you from the left and brings you to a stile. Cross the stile in the wall, enter the field and follow the right-hand wall to a gate in the far right-hand corner.

Through the gate a short enclosed lane is followed down to the road. Turn right between the buildings to a gate and stile and retrace your first steps to Lindale.

Walk 6   **5 miles**

Lyth Valley Hotel – Whitbarrow Scar – Row – Lyth

THIS WALK covers some 5 miles, much of it in delightful woodland as well as crossing a nature reserve and giving all round views that more than reward the slight climb involved. There are some slippery sections in wet weather.

The start is from the lay-by opposite the Lyth Valley Hotel on the A5074 Bowness to Gilpin Bridge/Levens road. Do not park on the hotel car park (grid ref. 453896 on OS SD48/58 Milnthorpe, which should be carried).

From the northern end of the lay-by an enclosed path starts on your left. Follow this up, keep right at the junction and carry straight on the access track which joins from the right. At the T junction by the cottage go right and follow the track through the woods.

After a straight stretch the track bends left and a gate gives you views of the Crinkles, Bowfell, Langdale Pikes, Fairfield, Red Screes and across to Scout Scar – a foretaste of what is to come.

Continue along the track and, after a gate, along the right-hand wall. This boundary is followed around the top end of the limestone scar.

A gate crosses your way and by now the Winster valley lies to your right and the Coniston fells are added to the landscape. Through the

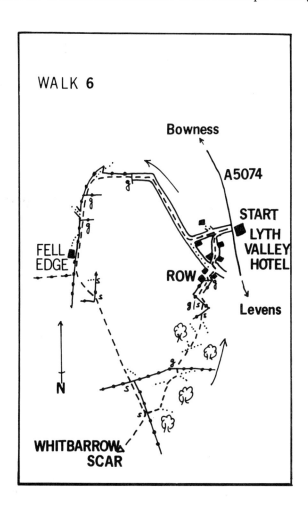

gate continue along the right-hand boundary although the path is narrower.

A track branches off right your way lies ahead through the gate. Continue along this boundary until you are above Field Edge Farm. Just after the farm an old hedge line comes up from below to meet your right-hand boundary. Here your path leaves the right-hand to begin to climb the escarpment on your left.

The climb is quite gentle and after some superb yew trees and springs (quite unique in limestone country) the path zig-zags before coming into more open land. Make half right on the top to meet the wall across your way on the left of an ash tree which itself is just short of the wall bend.

Between two short wooden posts is a stile and over continue half right (keeping some distance to the left of the dark, erratic boulders) to climb between the hillocks in a longish, shallow trough. This will lead you to a stile in a wall behind a larch tree. The woods will have been in sight for most of this last stretch.

Over the stile follow the path near the left-hand wall to which you will shortly return, Meanwhile continue along your path that climbs to the cairn that tops Lords Seat (Whitbarrow Scar).

The cairn is a memorial to Canon G.A.K. Hervey who was a founder of the Lake District, now Cumbria Wildlife Trust and one of whose reserves you are now on.

The 360° panorama from here needs a map to unfold all you can see.

Return down the last path to the stile in the wall which you now cross to find a path descending.

After some 200m, at a crude cairn, the path forks and you go left. Continue on this path, ignoring the first path off to the left, until you meet a track junction by the badger's paw signs.

Go left, through a gate in a wall, and continue along the wooded path to pass an enclosure of christmas trees on your right, to a track across your way and another badger's paw. Cross straight over to find a narrow path that runs down the ride in the trees.

After some 200m go right down a further narrow path, keepleft where another path joins and descend to a gap stile in a wall. Through go half right to cross an old damson orchard to a gate and stile.

Pass through here and turn left to follow near the left-hand wall to meet a further wall across your way. Go right to find an enclosed lane possibly with stiles, and later a gate on your left. The lane continues through this gate to the delightful hamlet of Row.

Turn right past the barn and then left up the tarmac road. Take the first lane off to the right and follow this all the way through the hamlet with views across the Lyth valley to Underbarrow Scar.

Turn left down an enclosed path when the track enters a gateway and then right at the next junction to follow down to your car.

Sizergh Castle – Brigsteer – Scout Scar – Sizergh

THE WOODLANDS are at their best in spring (daffodils and later bluebells) and in autumn. A clear day will enhance the extensive views from the scars.

Start from the lay-by on the A6 adjacent to the gatehouse north of Sizergh Castle – there is a corresponding lay-by on the opposite, southbound, side of the dual carriage (grid ref. 501879 on SD38/48 Milnthorpe; the SE Lake District Outdoor Leisure map will also be needed). Go along the gated drive from the house to meet the car park situated behind the castle.

With the car park on your left and your back to the castle, go to enter a lane which is gated and go along the lane over a rise and down to a gate. Through follow the track by the left-hand wall to a gate and then the stile by the second gate to reach a road.

Cross the road to the right of the footpath sign and go down a track inside a wood. Continue along the track after a stile and gate, keep left at the first junction and right at the next two. The track goes along parallel to the edge of the wood to reach a gate and stile which you cross.

Cross the field near the left hand boundary and soon go up a footpath sign and gate by a farmhouse with a single round chimney stack. Officially the path zig-zags by the far side of the field.

Go through the gate, cross the road and small farm enclosure and re-enter the fields by a further gate. Go left behind the buildings but turn right up the field when behind the farmhouse and by a small stream with a limestone scar ahead. Go to the top left-hand corner of the field and, through a gate, go right up an enclosed track-passing some remote cottages on the way.

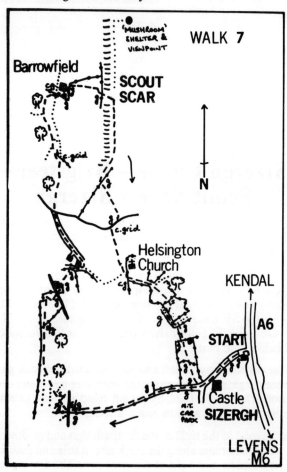

When the track opens out into a field, go left through a gate and down a track by the house. (Short cut up track to right to Helsington Church). Continue past house, down to a junction, keep right and follow the access track along through the woods to the road above Brigsteer.

Turn right along the road (short cut continue up road and go right at junction to church) and at the left-hand bend, turn left along the track (with footpath sign to Barrowfield). Continue to follow the track until it crosses a cattle-grid and enters a field.

Just before the cattle-grid a footpath sign leads you off left into the woods. Initially keep right near the wall on this narrow but mostly distinct path. Keep right at the first path junction and left at the junction shortly after. From then keep right until the path climbs slightly to re-meet the farm access road.

Go left on the road, over the cattle-grid and then turn right in front of the house and along to a gate. Through the gate a track leads behind the farm buildings and turns right up by a wall as it climbs towards the scar. Follow the track until it leads you to a gate in the stone wall ahead.

Through the gate the path climbs to the right as it ascends the scar. On the top the path becomes grassy and several paths lead to your right as you go along the scar, a wider path being slightly higher. The Scout Scar Mushroom lies to the left and, if you visit its viewpoint indicator, retrace your steps to where you emerged on the scar.

The view across the Lyth Valley to Whitbarrow Scar, across to the Coniston Fells, and the mountains of central and eastern Lakeland is a reward for the slight climb. Soon the views will open up to the Kent Estuary, the Arnside/Silverdale and Forest of Bowland AONBs and the Yorkshire Dales.

Continue along the scar south and soon a wall approaches from the left. Several paths lead down to a gate at the foot of this wall. Through take the distinct track across Helsington Barrows to a further gate and road. Turn right down the road and soon branch off left over the cattle-grid and along the track to the remote Helsington Church.

After the church is passed, a track goes left over a cattle-grid towards Berry Holme and its fine chimneys. Use this track to cross a field and, immediately after passing between two walls, leave the track to the right to descend a field with a small wood to the left.

Go down to a ladder stile in the boundary facing you and continue down to a gate in the wall behind the pole for overhead wires.

Through the gate go left down the track, through the gate facing you and then follow the right-hand wall to the next gate by a barn. Through this gate cross the next field on the distinct track and, after a further gate, another distinct track brings you to a gate by Sizergh Castle's car park.

The castle and its gardens are well worth a visit. If you parked by the A6 retrace your steps along the gated access drive.

Walk 8   **6 miles**
                                              (with shorter alternative)

Around Witherslack

A WALK for autumn when the trees are brown leaved and the fruits are ripe. An area of roe deer, red squirrels and usually a mewing buzzard – a walk through the woods.

Start from filling station and Little Chef resturant on A590 between Lindale and Levens. A lay-by near garage on east bound or by taking old road to rear of Derby Arms at Witherslack cars can easily be parked. Start at GR 439824 on OS Pathfinder map SD48/58 Milnthopre.

From the western side of the filling station a track goes to Catcrag Farm with a footpath sign to Halecat. Go along this track by the barn and pass on the left of the farm buildings to follow the track to pass through a gate.

Go the full length of the long narrow field to reach a stile in the stone wall across the narrow end of the field. Another stile, wooden, down to the left gives access to a steep path that drops to some limestone caves named Holy Well on the map.

Over the stone go ahead on a slight path and pick up a track on your left. Continue ahead on this track, going forward to a gate when another track crosses your way. Through here the track continues, mostly with a fence on your right, through woodlands of yew, hazel, blackthorn, elderberry, ash and crab apple. A definite autumn walk.

The track continues almost on top of a narrow limestone ridge until another gate crosses your way. Pass through this and the next gate in the right-hand corner of the field. A track then goes down behind the houses to the road.

Cross the road to steps and a footpath sign (Church) and follow its

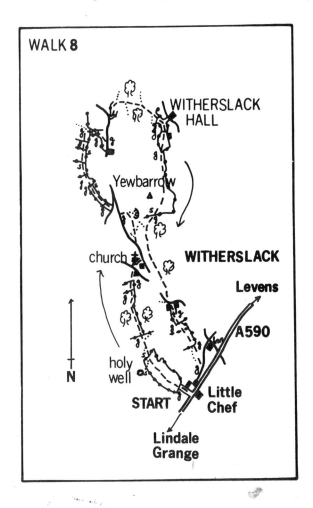

WALK 8

WITHERSLACK HALL

Yewbarrow

church

WITHERSLACK

Levens

A590

holy well

START

Little Chef

Lindale Grange

N

distinct line through the woods to pick up the left-hand wall. Some arrows guide you through the rear of the "Old Vicarage". On your left is St. Paul's Church of 1670 with a seat in the churchyard looking over to Cartmel Fell. Twelve yews in the yard are called the apostles.

A short cut can be found by using the footpath sign across the road and climbing to a path used later in the walk.

Go left down the road until it bends left. Leave it here by the ruined wall end and follow the distinct path through the woods, ignoring a path from the left and then one off to the right. Go along to meet the track to the small quarry. Go left down the track and then right down the road to the road junction (just beyond a large lime kiln in the woods on your left). Turn sharp left at the road junction and go down the road until a track leads off right (sign Low Wood).

Go down this track keeping to the enclosed track at the early double gate. Along the way the flat floor of the Winster Valley lies to your left beyond which lies Newton and Cartmel Fells. Yewbarrow lies to your right. The track ends by a gate and stile which you cross. Over the stile turn left and follow the right-hand hedge to another gate. Through this continue to cross a stile between two gates and then by the right-hand boundary to a stone stile in the wall near the field corner.

Go through the gate in the wall/fence junction facing you and then through the gate at the far right-hand corner of the field. Follow along the right-hand boundary until a track crosses your way. Turn right up the track, pass through the middle of three gates and up the enclosed track to pass through the next gate.

Continue in the same direction by a right-hand wall and wood and then at the end turn right to follow under the overhead wires to see a gate that admits you to the road.

Go left along the road and, after a field on your right, the road bends left. Ahead are views of the Lakeland fells. Leave the road to go along an enclosed track (sign Witherslack Hall) that initially skirts the edge of the wood as it climbs. Go straight across at the first junction and then keep to the maintrack as it climbs before bending right. Continue along this track to emerge at a gate with Witherslack Hall across a field to your left.

Through the gate turn right and follow the enclosed track to another gate through which your way lies half right across the field. This track goes by another gate into the wooded area and then swings left to follow the left-hand boundary.

After some distance, the wall swings away to the left near the end of the enclosure. Take the right-hand track that sweeps across the corner of Yewbarrow fell and re-meets a wall by a stile and gate.

Over the stile follow the distinct path, ignoring an early branch to the left. You pass through hazel thickets and bracken and darker areas by yew trees as the path gently descends towards Witherslack. On your way a path joins from your right – the short cut from the 'Old Vicarage'.

Follow your distinct track down until it meets the road. Go left on the road, ignore the footpath sign to Slate Hill, go round the bend and then right after the barn down a track (sign Latterbarrow) between a couple of houses to a gate.

Use this to re-enter the fields. Follow down near the right-hand boundary to a gate by an overhead wire pole. Through the gate bear left to follow the path that goes fairly straight through an area of scrub but never gets too far from the left-hand wall.

A gate will be found near the left-hand corner through which you enter a nature reserve of the Cumbrian Wildlife Trust. Continue along the path, bear left at the fork, and follow the grassy path down through this small but important limestone grassland reserve to a further gate and the old road. Turning right returns you to your start.

Walk 9   **5 miles**

Crook – Winster Valley – Crook

A PLEASANT walk through undulating but rocky countryside with many trees in the landscape. Long distance views of the Coniston fells, the Langdale Pikes and the Fairfield Horseshoe. Mostly on tracks, many old, so it is a walk that can be done after the wettest of weather – a suitable winter wander.

Just below the Wild Boar Inn, Crook a narrow road goes off Winster. A few cars may be parked here – only use the Inn Car Park if you have legitimate reason. The whole walk is on the OS SE Lakes Outdoor Leisure sheet and starts at grid ref. 435953.

Walk down this road, past Mitchelland Farm and continue uphill. Towards the top of the hill a track, Green Lane, goes off to the right. Follow this enclosed track over the ridge, and down, where it is tarred for a short section, to cross a metalled road before the final section of track leads you to the A5074.

Cross the road to a kissing gate and footpath sign (Gill Head) and follow the enclosed section into the open field, Go left here, a bridleway sign says GHYLL Head, and follow along a track by the left-hand wall, through two old gateways, and eventually to a gate

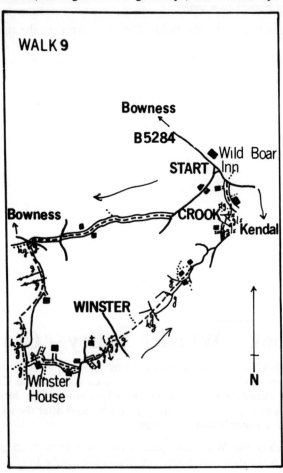

across your way. Go through this gate and the one shortly after and then continue along the left-hand wall to pick up a more distinct track which you follow to your right.

The track meanders away from and back towards the wall, keep left when a less distinct track goes right, following the ruined right-hand wall until a gate and kissing gate cross your path.

Through again follow the track by the left-hand wall but go left through the first gate to follow the distinct, enclosed track down to a further gate and kissing gate above Winster House.

Through the gate go right to pass in front of the house and follow its accrss track, passing Birket House to your left. Go along this track and up to meet the metalled road.

Go left along the road but just after Bryan Houses, and a short distance short of Winster Church, go right down the enclosed bridleway, signposted Crag Lane, making sure to go through the gate on the left by the farm outbuilding.

Through the gate follow the track, once enclosed, to eventually pass through a gate, down to cross the stream, up through a further gate and then along the left-hand wall to climb through the field to a further gate and road.

Cross the road directly to a further gate and bridleway sign. In the large enclosure, follow the track up to reach a gate and kissing gate, through which you descend to a further gate, by following the old track, in the lowest part of the field. Continue along the track to the gate by the barn. Through this gate go right to pass Thorneyfields, bear left at the houses and then right at the next junction.

Over the stream with the road climbs, keep right at the first junction and then go left when the larger road is reached. Continue uphill but go left along the first track, at Shepherd's Yeat.

Go along the drive but continue ahead through the gate and stile when the track bends left to the house. Go to the barn, keep to the right of the gate and follow the left-hand wall and fence to a small gate. Through this continue by the ruined left-hand wall until a wooden stile in front of a stone gap stile can be crossed.

In the field go to the gate and stile to the right of the trees and then half left to a gap stile. In this last field, follow the right-hand wall up to a gate and stile which give access to a track which, if followed left, will return you to your starting point.

Staveley in Cartmel – Cartmel Fell – Staveley

THIS IS an 8 mile walk on the map but one that can feel more like 10 because of the twists and turns and ups and downs. It is worthwhile to take a full day and to spend some time visiting Cartmel Fell Church as well as finding many delightful viewpoints and restpoints along the way. It is a walk that cannot be rushed and the underfoot terrain suggests boots should be worn. The effort, after the initial forest section, will be well rewarded with a good Lakeland day out walking.

Start one mile east of Newby Bridge where side road goes off to Staveley. You can park in several places around here at the lower end of Chapel House Plantation (grid ref. 383852 on OS SD28/38 Broughton and Newby Bridge; SD48/58 Milnthorpe will also be needed).

Start where the forest road enters the plantation (with a footpath sign). Follow the road upwards until it goes round a left-hand bend. Look for, and join, a green path on your right by a clump of darker pines (against the background of larch). The green path climbs and a ruined wall meets the wall on your right. Keep alongside this wall until a path crosses your way over the rise, with the forest road visible down to your left.

Turn right along the path, go through a gap in the wall and the green path soon goes into darker trees. You soon emerge at a T-junction of paths with the forest road again down to the left. Turn right and follow the path up the groove.

When the path levels out there is a footpath sign – your way is straight ahead (Hare Hill) and gently downwards to rejoin the forest road which you follow to the right.

Continue along the road until it bends left when you can go along a green track directly ahead – the junction coming just after passing a small tarn down to your right. The track passes through some more open and deciduous birch trees before going to the edge of the forest and a stile.

Over the stile, cross the field in the direction of the vehicle tracks

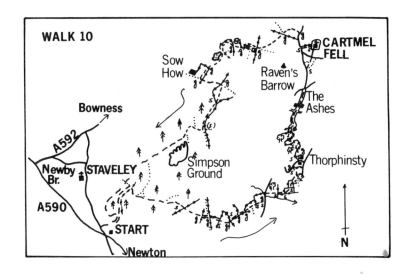

Sow
How

Bowness

Newby
Br.

STAVELEY

A590

A592

START

Newton

Simpson
Ground

Raven's
Barrow

CARTMEL
FELL

The
Ashes

Thorphinsty

N

and then go through the gate in the wall on the far side of the field. In the next, short field, follow the right hand wall to meet a farm access track. Directly cross the track, go through the right-hand of two gates and then follow the left-hand wall to the corner of the field. Cross the stile facing you in the corner and then cross the next field, above the rushes, to the obvious gate.

Through the gate go left to the field corner and cross the wall stile on your right. In the field go down near the right-hand ditch and fence to a gate in the wall that crosses your way – go through.

On the way down the field you have a wide vista of the eastern fells of Lakeland, the Howgills, the Yorkshire Dales and Ingleborough and with Witherslack and the Winster Valley more initmate below you.

Go down the next field parallel to the right-hand fence and then pass through the lowest gate in the wall across your way. Through the gate a track leads down but when it bends right go straight on, down a depression in the field and find a stone stile to your right in the wall by an overhead wire pole.

Over the last stile you now have to descend a steep and rocky field – pick your way carefully – to a stile between the gate and overhead wire pole, over which you join the road and go left.

Just over the bridge a footpath sign on your right (Crag Wood) takes you off the road and down through a wood to a stile. Over the stile follow the ruined fence to a further stile in a newly planted enclosure. Go half left through the newly planted trees (roughly between the white and the brown grow tubes) to a further stile in the left-hand boundary. Over this stile cross the field to the far right hand corner where a tall stile over a deer fence admits you again into a wood.

Go half left gently down the wood (and brambles) to meet a path contouring across. This path lead you left and then up to a stile by a gate and an overhead wire pole mounted transformer and gives access to a road.

Go right and down the road to Thorphinsty Hall Farm. On the road-bend go to the left and keep all the farm buildings, including some massive stone barns, to your right. On the left of the last stone barn there is a stile found by climbing the small banking.

Over the stile cross the field parallel to the left-hand wall, pass the rocky outcrop and large holly and then descend to a stream and gate. Through the gate follow the track ahead in this ancient woodland until a track crosses your way with two separate clumps of trees in grow tubes (3 and 15 in number) on your left. Turn right here but then climb to the left of the next clump of three grow tubes to reach a stile after passing through further newly planted trees.

Use the stile to gain access to the field and cross this to the stone gap stile in the wall ahead and re-enter a wood. A short path leads through the wood to a stile. Cross and then follow the right-hand fence to the far right-hand corner of the field. Cross here and go ahead and then right to drop down to the access road of Little Thorphinsty. Go left along the access road and continue ahead over the cattle-grid to pass 'The Ashes' and eventually reach the road at a junction.

Go straight across the road signposted Bowness and the Church and follow the road until a stile and footpath sign on your right admit you to some rough ground. Follow the path that initially keeps up then, after a depression, climbs to the road where you cross to go down the signed access track to the church.

The church is a wonderful corner of Cumbria with much of interest especially when daffodils clothe the graveyard. A guide book can be purchased in the church for a nominal sum and is well worth using to conduct you around this historic and peaceful building.

Going out of the church porch go right, pass the tower and up to a stile in the top corner of the churchyard. Through this follow the right-hand wall to meet the road which you follow to the right.

Follow the tarmac until when the road descends a gate on your left, just before two pole-mounted triangular road signs, re-admits you to the fields. Through the gate follow the track upwards until, when it is near the left-hand wall, a branch from the track takes you through into the next field where you continue to follow the track up and over the ridge of the field. Away to your left is a prominent cairn, Raven's Barrow, marked as a memorial on you OS map.

The track meanders over the field but eventually meets another track from the left and goes down to a gate on the right hand side of the small plantation of rhododendrons. Through this gate follow the wood-site path ahead and along to the right-hand side of the barn. Go right and follow the track beside the left-hand wall – this then bends back left and takes you above the barn and then along the field to a gate and a track into the wood.

Follow the distinct track to a shed where a footpath sign shows where the path and bridleway diverge. Go right along the distinct footpath, pass the end of the delightful Middle Tarn and then round to a gate and back into the field. In the field follow the distinct line of the track ahead and below the right-hand boundary until a derelict wall coming down the field is met above the boathouse and quiet Sow How Tarn. Go left to follow the wall down to a gateway where you go right – having just rejoined the bridlepath.

The track goes over the outlet stream of the tarn, along to a gate and then up a field to meet another track at a T-junction to the left of Sow How Farm. Go left on this track, pass through the first gate, down the track and through the second gate. Leave the track, to the right, in this field and follow, by a footpath sign, the right-hand wall until it bends away to the right. Take the gently sloping way across to your left and continue upwards to pass under the overhead wire and then reach a stile in the far corner of the field.

Over the stile follow the left-hand wall with the forest on your right until a stile in the wall and a marked path goes off to the right. Follow this path, ignoring rides off to the right and a track of to the left near the dam of Simpson Ground Reservoir which can be glimpsed, and a worthwhile visit can be made, until it ends by a junction of tracks just short of the forest road. Go ahead along the forest track and then road. Keep right and down when you shortly meet the main forest road. This will return you to your starting point.

Ashes Lane – Cunswick Scar – Gamblesmire – Ashes Lane

A PLEASANT walk through fields, a climb of Cunswick Scar with wide-ranging views and along some old tracks that missed becoming metalled roads.

Start between Kendal and Staveley on the A591, the road climbs over a rise with dual carriageway. Signposted off to the west is Ashes Lane caravan site. Access to Ashes Lane is off the loop of the old main A591 – there is plenty of parking space, particularly towards the bottom of this loop, GR 495965 on the SE Lakes Outdoor Leisure sheet which should be carried.

Towards the bottom of the old road is a signpost by a stile to Ratherheath. The path goes through a wood, crosses Ashes Lane to climb a stile and gate (signposted to Bonning Gate) and re-enters a wood. Follow the distinct track through the plantation to emerge in the fields by a gate on the far side by Ratherheath Tarn. Go round the right-hand side of the field by the wood fence to cross a stile between two wooden uprights in the wall that crosses your way.

In the next field climb to the left and then go diagonally right down the length of the field to gain the road by a stile besides a footpath sign near the far right-hand corner of the field. This length will be walked in reverse if you take the short cut.

Go left on the road, pass the track to two bungalows on your right and at the end of the next field go right through a gate and follow the track alongside the left hand boundary to a gateway and the entrance to Moss Side house. Go to the left of the garden wall and then go diagonally left to go through a gate at the far end of the wall in the left-hand field boundary.

Go half right in the next field to cut the field corner and pass a gate and then go along the right-hand hedge and then pass through the gate in the wall. Climb the field below Bank End house and go to a gate on the right of the house, through which you follow the access road to the right until it bends right by a plantation.

Leave the road by the imposing but unnecessary stile to regain the fields. Follow the right-hand hedge to a stone stile facing you, over which you cross the next field and pass through the gate directly opposite the stile. In this field go right to follow the hedge to reach the road by the stile and gate.

Cross the road directly and gain access to the fields by the gas stile (to Cunswick Scar). Cross the field to gain a further gap stile at the bottom corner of the wooded area. In this area go to the stile behind

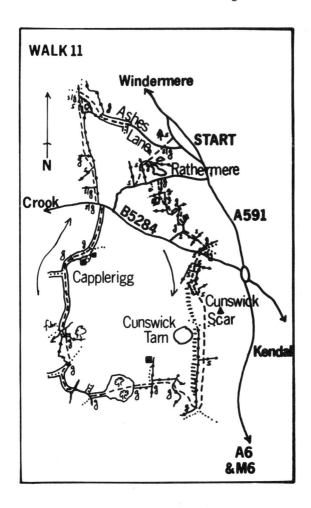

the big tree and then follow the distinct and waymarked path that gently rises to reach a stile at a fence corner on more open land.

Over this stile follow the right-hand fence and then cross the stile in the top corner to give access to the open fell above the scar. The highest point is to your left and views of the Lakeland Fells, the Howgills, the edge of the Yorkshire Dales and the fells of the Forest of Bowland are in view. Cunswick tarn can be seen below the scar.

Your way now follows the edge of the steep scar along a faintly defined path that descends gently to a col. Ignore the stile on the right and continue by the right-hand fence and then wall, cross a stile in a fence across your way and, climbing gently, you come to a footpath sign at a wall corner under the overhead power lines.

Go right and right through the gate (signposted Gamblemire Lane). The distinct lane descends passing a lime kiln to a gate. Continue along with the boundary on your right to a further gate through which you ignore the track off right to Cunswick Hall Farm and continue along the track by the left-hand wall. The lane then goes through a further gate ahead to descend through an old wood and emerge as a track enclosed by hedges.

The way ahead is now distinct but somewhat undulating. When the track comes to a gate go through and turn right along the metalled road, ignore the right turn to Cold Harbour Farm as you continue over the cattle-grid, over the hillock and down to a junction. Your way lies directly ahead on the enclosed green lane.

Over the hillock the land comes down to a junction where you go right, pass through the gate and continue ahead until the wall on the left bends down left. Take the left fork in the track that descends to the bottom of a wood where you have to pass through a gate to regain an enclosed track.

Follow this track to your left, it crosses a stream by a footbridge and then climbs to a track junction by a sign. Go right even though there is no sign pointing this way, and continue left through the gate at the far end of the drive to Capplerigg. Follow the farm access to the main road.

For a short cut, go right and immediately left until you find the stile you previously crossed on the outward leg and from where you can retrace your steps.

Continue by turning left on the main road, cross and find a stile by a gate (signed Ashes Wood and Staveley). Use these to gain access to the fields where you follow the right-hand wall through three consecutive fields using the stiles facing you each time.

In the fourth field go to the left of the reeds, pass a lone ash tree and then go ahead to pass through a gate in the wall facing you. In the next field start by gradually going to meet the right-hand wall and then following this towards Ashes Wood. When you meet the wood turn left to follow the short-fenced section and then right to follow the wall between the field and the wood.

Part way down this wall is a crag and then a ladder stile over which you follow the path down through the wood to a stile and gate. In this next field go by the left-hand wall to the footpath sign and then turn right to follow the track (not signed) which is the continuation of Ashes Lane. After the field the track becomes enclosed, you pass through a gate and after the caravan site the tarmacadamed road will lead you back to where you started.

Walk 12   **7½ miles**

Crook Church – Crosthwaite – Underbarrow – Crook

START by Crook Church on B5284 Kendal – Bowness road (some cars can be parked at the memorial hall if not in use). Likewise starting at Crosthwaite church (but no parking during services) and this makes the route ½ mile less. Parking at Underbarrow is very difficult and not recommended. Crook Church is grid ref. 451951 on the SE Lakes Outdoor Leisure sheet which should be carried.

From Crook Memorial Hall go down the road towards the church to find a kissing gate on the right of two gates on your left (opposite the drive to Yew Tree Farm). Follow the track up the field to meet the wall corner and then turn right to follow the above wall to the ruined tower and yard of the original St Catherine's church.

The old church is supposed to date to c1620 but Pevsner believes the bell openings and parapet look Jacobean. The new church is dated 1887. The fourteenth century bell was transferred to the new church. An old gravestone remains to be seen in the enslosed yard. The old church is the subject of a poem by local poet Margaret Cropper.

With your back to the gate into the churchyard, go half right to meet the wall, cut the corner as it drops away, and then cross the stile in the wall. Go down the left-hand wall but, on reaching the gate, turn right to follow the track across the field, along an old boundary and then under the overhead wires. Leave the track here and cut across to pass through the gate behind the pole of the next set of overhead wires and enter the next field.

Go along the right-hand wall but at the second gateway in the wall turn left to cross the widest part of the field to a stile and gate to the left of the wood. Over the stile contour across the field to ignore the first gate on your right but to cross the fence where a distinct track leads over the next field.

Follow this track as it gently cimbs and leads, via a series of gates and fields, to the yard of Low Fold Farm. Bear left in the yard to go down the farm access track as far as the junction at the end of the enclosed section.

Turn right at the junction but, after a short distance, go left to cross the ladder stile in the approaching left-hand wall before the next gate. In the next field, go ahead parallel to the right-hand wall to pass between knolls as you climb the field. At the far end skirt round the left of the damp hollow, below the steep left-hand ridge, to cross a stile in the boundary facing you.

Follow the right hand boundary, but skirt the damp area to its left, and continue over the hill and begin to descend along the wall until a distinct stoney path begins to lead you away from the wall – the wall itself begins to veer to pass a small knoll. Follow the stony track until it peters out and then continue down this large, rough intake by aiming for a gate where a wall and fence abutt across the intake. Go through the gate, start along the vehicle track to the left but cut diagonally down this rough field to a gate near the bottom left-hand corner. The gate is below a line of old thorn trees, once part of a hedge, and above some deer fencing.

The views ahead encompass the Kent estuary, the back of Whitbarrow Scar and the Winster Valley.

Once through the gate, go right down the enclosed track, turn left along the road at the bottom, go left at the junction and continue to the next road junction set amongst the attractive cottages of this detached part of Crosthwaite.

The next short section involves a miriad of small fields but, with care, the obvious stiles will cause little problem. Cross the junction to enter the drive of Fern Lea house. Go by the right-hand side of the house and follow the boundary around and down to a stile by a gate – the white bungalow and outbuildings are to the right.

In the field, cross the middle to a slab footbridge and through the

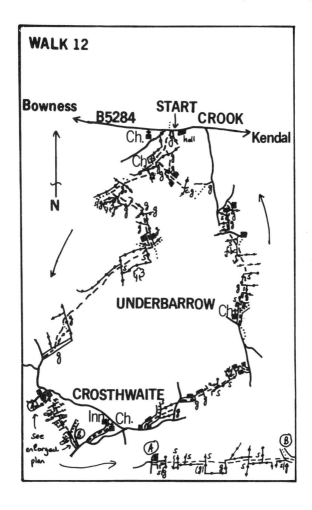

obvious gap stile in the wall facing you. In the next field, follow the right-hand wall, cross the stile facing you, continue along the right-hand wall and then cross the wall ahead (with a gate on your right). Cross the next field to the obvious gateway and then follow the left-hand wall to cross the gap stile in the corner. Walk along the right-hand wall to pass through a further stone gap stile where the hedge line meets the wall. In this last field, walk near the right-hand wall continuing, after the gap and the corner that sticks out, to go to a stile and gate which give you access to an enclosed lane.

Go right down the lane, left at the junction along the road, but after 20 metres turn left up the enclosed lane that climbs up to Crosthwaite Church and the Punch Bowl Inn.

To continue, go to the road above the church, turn right but bear left on the main road at the junction and continue along the road to pass the Crosthwaite parish road sign.

Cross the road to the left and go up the track to the left of Rose Bank. Follow the track up to pass the terrace of cottages and continue to just before it makes a sharp left turn, where the track widens, to cross a stile in the wall on your right. In the field, go down the middle of the long length to pass through a gate on the far side that gives access to a road.

Go left on the road but turn right when it bends left to go past the group of houses at Blakebank. Walk down the lane, through the gate that gives access to Middle Blakebank, and continue down the lawn at the front of the house to pass through the gate by the outbuilding.

In the field, follow the left-hand boundary, continuing in this direction when the track follows the old hedge line and descends the narrow ridge to an enclosed section at the end of the field. At the end of this section cross through the stile between the two left-hand gates and then follow the right-hand wall over the field to find, and cross, a stone gap stile in the hedged section of the boundary that crosses your way. In the next field, contour round the left hand slope to a stile by a gate, over which a track leads down and through the farmyard of Kirkby House to eventually cross over Chapel Beck to reach the road.

Go left on the road, keeping left at the junction, to pass through part of Underbarrow, and arrive at the church which, according to Pevsner, has a "naughty" design. Take the track on the immediate right of the church and yard. Follow this track along, pass through the gateposts on the left of the bungalow (Lynwood) and then reach the group of properties at Chapel House.

On your left is Chapel Spring Cottage and to the right of the entrance gate, hidden behind a pole, is a gap stile which you use to enter the fields. From the stile go right and pick up the left-hand boundary. In the corner of the field pass through the left-hand of two gateways and then turn right to follow the right-hand wall to pass through the next gateway. Cross the next field to a stile in the top left-hand corner, over which you follow above the wooded edge of Chapel Beck and pass two broken walls that cross your way.

After here Beckside Farm comes into view. Continue in the same direction until a footbridge, and subsequent stile, enable you to cross the beck on your left. In the next, rough field go half right as you pick your way to a stile in the fence some 60 metres above the beck and under some overhead wires. Continue over the stile in the same direction to cross the remainder of the field and the farm access to find a stile where the wall bends slightly away from the track edge to reach a small beck.

Through this stile follow the right-hand wall, pass through a gateway, continue along by the wall to find a gap stile where the fence comes down to the wall. Go over the stile, along the left-hand wall, through the gate and continue up the concrete access road.

When you reach the road go left but then right at the next junction to climb steeply up the road. At its highest point a gate on the left gives access to a track to Crook Hall. Go through the gate, follow the track– keeping right at the junction, all the way up to and through the yard of Crook Hall Farm. The track stops at a series of gates.

If you started at Crosthwaite then go through the left-hand gate, cross the field to the next gate and reach the tower of St Catherine's old Church.

If you began at Crook then go through the right-hand gate and follow the track down to the next gate, through which the track continues down to your starting point.

Bowness – School Knott – Crook – Brant Fell – Bowness

AN undulating walk in the countryside east of Bowness, with several good viewpoints. Inexperienced walkers should take care in the section around School Knott on a day of low mist. Start at Bowness by the boat landings, grid ref. 402967 on the SE Lakes Outdoor Leisure series map.

Leave the boatlandings and walk up Lake Road, passing the Old England Hotel, St Martin's Church and keep right on the A5074 at the junction by the Albert Hotel.

Soon you climb to the Lakeland Sheepskin Centre where you turn right up Helm Road, pass the Windermere Hydro Hotel, and continue up until the road bends sharply up to the left. Just on the left, and worth the extra effort, is Biskey How viewpoint. your way lies straight on, through the old gate posts and ignoring any turns left or right until you see a notice 'Cul de Sac to Helm Farm' which you follow all the way above the houses to reach the old (1691), interesting, white Helm Cottage farmhouse.

To the left of the cottage is a kissing gate before a gate on your left through which you cross a short field on a path, through the next kissing gate and then keep by the right-hand fence to cross a stone gap stile.

Through this stile go right and up the enclosed path at the rear of the bungalows until you come to a path junction by a signpost. Go right, through the wall gap, and climb to the right to reach the right-hand side of the highest house at the top of the field.

Enter the field by the house, follow the left-hand wall past the former farmhouse and then continue along the grooved path to a kissing gate by a gate in the top right-hand corner of the field. Pass through this, cross the road and then climb the stile fancing you.

In the next field, follow the right-hand wall along and down. When it bends right near the bottom of the field, bear right and go above the left-hand boundary to a stile visible ahead. Cross the stile and

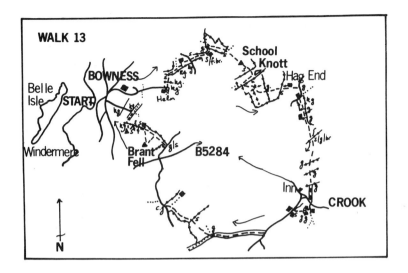

footbridge, climb the steps and go left along the track to pass the front of Old Droomer house and then continue to pass through a gate.

Turn right in the field and make your way up to cross a stile in the top left-hand corner over which you make your way ti the highest point of School Knott ahead. Although only 232m (760 feet) high this little rocky fell offers worthwhile views.

With your back to the way you came, go ahead to find a faint track down to a stile in a gateway and beyond School Knott Tarn which you reach by the right hand extremity. Turn right and go along the left-hand wall until, some 40m short of the gate in the field corner, you will find a gap in the left-hand wall by four larch trees.

Go through the gap and bear half left to climb the field to reach a junction of ruined walls in the top left-hand corner. Go ahead through the ruined wall gap just to the left of an isolated ash tree in the wall you cross. Walk ahead and gently down the slope to the damp depression on your left. Bear left to skirt this depression on its right-hand side to find a path that becomes increasingly more obvious as it descends via a gateway, over a small beck and down to cross a stile.

43

In this next field, follow the broken left-hand wall to pass through to the yard and down the access track of the former Hay End Farm complete with it remnants of scrap etc.,

At the metalled road go right and pass through old gate posts and a gate by Outrun Nook. Ignore the first footpath sign on your left (Borwick Fold) and go through the kissing gate by the second sign (Dales Way) also on your left.

Climb the field to pass a rocky outcrop and then climb to pass through a gate in the top left-hand corner of the field. Follow this left-hand wall to pass by Crag House and descend to cross through the right-hand of three adjacent gates at the lowest part of the enclosure.

In the large field follow the track down to the infant Gilpin Beck but keep to the nearside of the beck to reach a gate and stile. This rough field contains some fine holly trees.

Cross the stile and the beck and then climb along the track up a short rise, Continue along the track that roughly follows the beck to pass through three gates before an enclosed track brings you to the B5284 at Crook. The Wild Boar Hotel lies to your right.

Continue by crossing the road diagonally left and then bearing right to Hole Farm at the junction below the cottages. Pass the house and stone barn and then bear slightly left before going ahead between the newer buildings through the gated yard.

Re-enter the fields and follow the overhead wires down to a stile by the beck. Over this and the footbridge go left along the road and climb the hill. Near the crest, leave the road to go right up the enclosed Green Lane. This lane is followed for some distance and you leave it by the second gate on your right (with limestone gateposts).

In the large rough field go ahead, ignore the track to the right, and slowly descend to cross the width of the field to a ladder stile some 100m up from the bottom left-hand corner of the field and on the right of a fairly permanent pool.

Use the stile to cross into the next field which you cross by aiming for the white houses and gradually meet the left-hand wall. On a knoll the wall bends away left but just beyond the knoll you find a farm access track and to the left a gate and cattle-grid and access to a minor road.

Go right along the minor road, cross the B5284, and continue along the minor road (signed Heathwaite). At the end of the wood on your left, a track goes left to a stile and gate. Cross the stile and follow the track towards Brantfell Farm.

If you wish to climb Brant Fell for its fine views and, for young children, some excellent scrambling on the summit rocks, then climb left up the open fellside. To continue drop down to the track again and continue along towards the farm.

The track reaches a gate above the farm. On the nearside of the gate go left along and up by the right-hand wall until there is a stone stile in the wall by the fence. Cross this, follow the left-hand wall down to the next stile which is, along with the stile immediately after, crossed.

Go ahead in the field to the highest knoll, called Post Knott, for another viewpoint then go through the kissing gate by the gate to your right. Go left down the track until, just after the woods ends, you find a kissing gate by a gate on your left (another one on the right). Go through and follow the path down the field to a gate at the bottom. The road beyond leads down to your start in Bowness.

Bowland Bridge – Wood Farm – – Hubbersty Head – Bowland Bridge

A WALK of delight along the Winster Valley – especially at daffodil and blossom time, some delightful woodlands and chances to see wildlife. Start at the Hare and Hounds Inn, Bowland Bridge (grid ref. 418897 on SD48/58; the SE Lakes Outdoor Leisure map will also be needed). The return is down the small dale of the Winster tributary, Arndale Beck.

From the hotel go to cross Bowland Bridge and the Winster, once the Westmorland – Lancashire boundary, to a stile on your right (fp sign Hollins Farm). In the field, cross to the wood and enter by the large oak tree on the boundary. Climb the rise behind the tree and then cross to the left of a rock slab and leave the wood in the wall gap where the two derelict stone walls meet.

Follow the left-hand wall up the field but when you reach the buildings turn right to pass under the overhead wires to use a stone gap stile in the hedge across the field. Go across the field and through the gate beyond the overhead wire pole and then follow the left-hand wall to gain access to a gap stile by the house.

Once over the stile, cross the garden and go right to the gate between the two barns after which you follow the track down the field to pass through a further gate. Continue along and go through the right-hand of two gate ways. Continue on the enclosed track and then in the following field by the right-hand wall to a further gate and small beck beyond to cross.

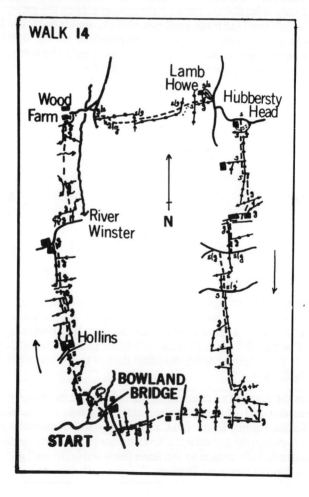

Go through the field to pass through the gate in the top left-hand corner and then follow the track up to a further gate which gives you access to the road. Go right and downhill on the road and enter the left-hand wood at its lowest point (fp sign Wood Farm). Use the track along the wood boundary and then pass through a gate into a field. Leave by the gate in the short enclosed track after crossing via the lowest of the overhead wire poles.

In this larger field, head for the prominent wall corner and cross the beck to the left of the overhead wire pole to reach it. Continue to pass through the gate ahead (under the wires) and then cross to pass through the next gate. This gives access to a track which you follow right to the barn and then continue right along the access track (to Wood Farm) to recross the Winster and reach the road.

Go right along the road but cross to the stile by the first gate on your left. (fp sign Lamb Howe). This gives access to a track which you follow up to pass through a kissing gate by a gate in the right-hand wall. In the next wooded pasture the track bends slightly left and is followed to a gate and stile. Over the stile follow the track by the right-hand fence and then cross the next stile by a gate when the fence crosses your way. From here, go ahead on the track to climb a slight rise, another track joins from the right, and then down to cross a stile in a gate.

In the field make for the gate to the right of the house and go through to follow the left hand wall by two further gates adjacent to the house to gain the access track. Go right down the track and right along the road at the bottom.

Take the first left fork (Hubbersty Head) and climb up the road to find a stile on your right immediately after the first house (Mearson's Farm). Cross this, drop down the enclosure, cross the access track and then the stile in the far wall.

In the field, go to the overhead pole where three wires meet and then follow the left-hand hedge down to cross a stone stile in the short section of wall facing you. The Damson Dene Hotel lies across to your right. Continue along the left-hand hedge in the next field but look for, and cross, a stone stile in the hedge. Go by the right-hand hedge in this field, through a gate at the bottom and then through a series of gates facing you to reach the farm outbuildings.

Turn right in the yard and follow the track until you can branch left before the next gate across your way. Climb this field and then follow the right-hand boundary down through a gate and reach the road by a stile by the next gate.

Go right on the road but cross to a stile by a gate behind the road signpost. Use this to enter the field and climb directly ahead, cross a stile in the wall that crosses your way (between two gates). Follow the right-hand wall down this next field with views of Whitbarrow Scar ahead and then cross the stile by the gate and then the road diagonally right to a stone slab gap stile to the right of the gate.

In the fields again, follow the left-hand wall but then descend to the pass through the second gate from the left – some 20m from the corner. Climb the hillock ahead to cross the stile where the wall meets the hedge and then follow the straggling left-hand hedge to cross a stone gap stile in the far right-hand corner of the field.

Follow the left-hand wall down the field, pass the small angular corner and then go left through the gate in the next section of wall. Go over the bridge and turn right to cross the field and then the wooden stile in the wall that descends the field.

Cross the next field towards the top left-hand corner but, on the near side of the gate, turn right and follow the track down by the wall, through the gate at the bottom. Continue across the next field, over the stile by the next gate and then across Arndale Beck and through the subsequent gate. In the next field, go to pass through the double gate and reach the road.

Cross the road diagonally left to a stile in the wall and in the field go by the right-hand side of the barn and then go in the direction of the overhead wires to cross a ladder stile, by a pole, in the next wall across your way.

Follow the right-hand wall through two fields to a wooden stile in the far right-hand corner of the second field. This stile crosses you diagonally into the next field where you follow the left-hand wall along, over a broken wall and to a stile and the road. Your start is just to your right.